Birthday Bash!

Other Books by Dan Reynolds

The Toilet Zone: A Hilarious Collection of Bathroom Humor
Christmas Meltdown

Birthday Bash!

A Reynolds Unwrapped Party . . .

DAN REYNOLDS

**Andrews McMeel
Publishing**

Kansas City

Birthday Bash!

www.reynoldsunwrapped.com
e-mail: dreynol3@twcny.rr.com

ISBN: 0-7407-1413-9

02 03 04 05 06 TWP 10 9 8 7 6 5 4 3 2 1

Library of Congress Control Number: 2001096658

Attention: Schools and Businesses

Andrews McMeel books are available at quantity discounts
with bulk purchase for educational, business, or sales promo-
tional use. For information, please write to: Special Sales
Department, Andrews McMeel Publishing, 4520 Main Street,
Kansas City, Missouri 64111.

This book is not only about birthdays and growing older—it is about staying young. I'd like to dedicate this book to my children . . . Gregory, Ronnie, Johnnie, and my fourth child who is en route. The first thing you learn after having children is you *need* a sense of humor. It is with the help of my children that I am able to keep my own inner child young and full of laughter. I hope as they grow older, they will remember this thought . . . if they only have two cents left to their names—make sure one of them is a sense of humor.

I love you all so much.

FOREWORD

What can you say about a guy whose main goal in life is to draw funny pictures and make others laugh? It is either a healthy outlet for artistic expression or a demented form of cheap therapy.

Personally, I believe Dan Reynolds falls somewhere in between. He has that rare ability that every successful cartoonist must posses . . . the gift to see humor in the most unlikely of places and point it out for all the world to see.

But rather than ramble on about how funny, bright, witty, etc., Dan's cartoons are, I'd prefer to pay him the highest compliment I know. It's a thought I've had many times while perusing his work (though it's usually said out of frustration): "Damn, I wish I'd thought of that!"

—Leigh Rubin
Creator of *Rubes*

For you on your birthday:
THE TOP 10
OXYMORONS

10. junk food
9. postal service
8. old news
7. legally drunk
6. diet ice cream
5. tight slacks
4. pleasantly plump
3. plastic silverware
2. twelve-ounce pound cake

and the #1 oxymoron...
Happy Birthday

"Surprise!"

Nerd birthday party games

Happy birthday
from all of us
to all of you.

Elephant mid-life crisis

Janet wishes for a body
her friends could only
dream of having.

Cat gag gifts

Beetle birthdays

The moment prior
to Bozo's conception

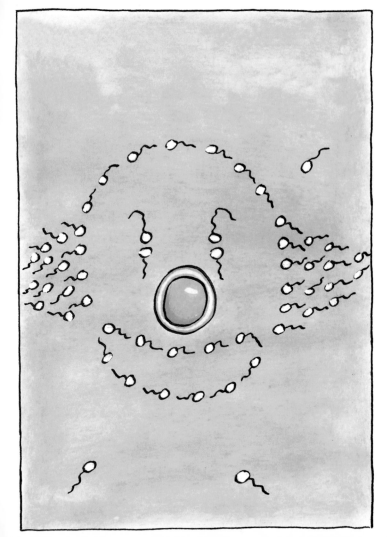

"Hey, this isn't birthday cake . . .
it's cow pie!"

"No, no . . . I mean't 'cut the cake'!"

knuckles mistakenly wishes
for a cake in a file.

How aging affects belt height

YOUTH ADULT MIDDLE- OLD
AGE AGE

The birth of Ma Bell

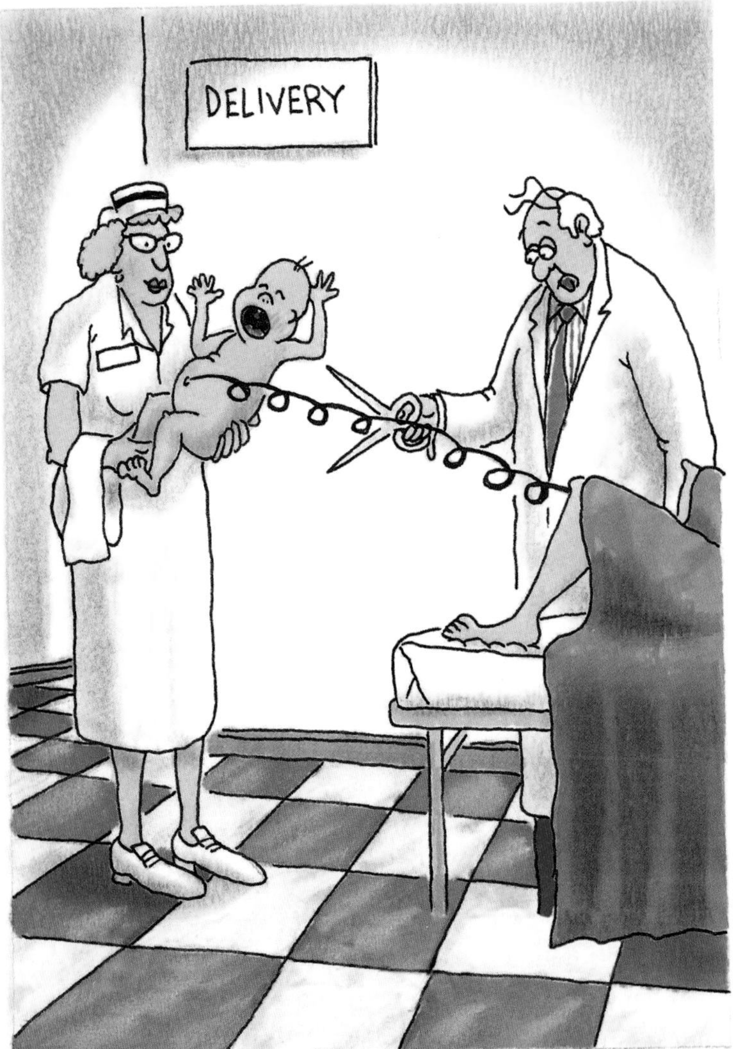
DELIVERY

"Surprise!"

How aging affects your
philosophy of life

CHILD

TEEN

MID-LIFE

OLD AGE

Maximum Insecurity Prison
for Women

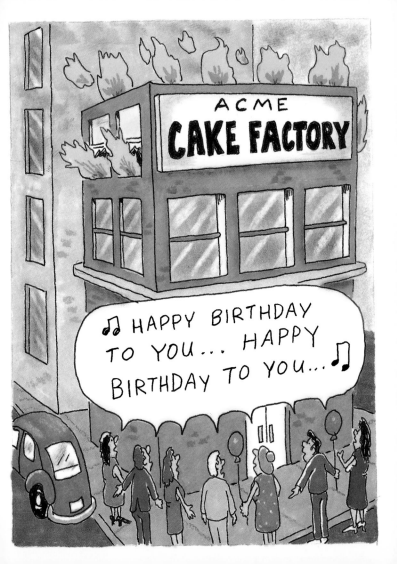

The new, parent-approved
Barney piñata

The room fell silent.
Someone thought they heard
a pin drop.

"You're forty years old."

Beware of geeks bearing gifts.

Redneck birthday games

Pin the Donkey on the Tail

Birthday Support Group

HAPPY BIRTHDAY